WHILE
WAITING
for CHANGE

What happens to you
while you're trying to
change them and Waiting
for them to Change?

By Cecilia Thomas

xulon
PRESS

While Waiting For Change
(What happens to you while you're trying to change them and Waiting for them to Change?)
by Cecilia Thomas

Printed in the United States of America.

ISBN 9781498466585

www.xulonpress.com

NOTES OF THANKS AND DEDICATION

Thank you God

This book is dedicated to the memory of
my father and mother
DAVID AND MARGUERITE THOMAS

SPECIAL THANKS TO:
Thanks to all my family (sisters and all relatives)
friends, sisters and brothers in Christ for the part
you have all played in my life!
Betty A. Gilmore
Merridy, Ron and Gail Aggen
YWCA NorthEasternNY
(Executive and all Directors)
H.O.P.E. Enterprises
Mary May-LCSW

ALSO TO:
Bishop Clarence Keaton, R.I.P
And the memory of all family and friends who
have passed on, R.I.P.

I LOVE YOU ALL!

WHILE WAITING FOR CHANGE

While waiting for change,
I'm praying and fasting.
While waiting for change,
Enduring and long-suffering.
While waiting for change,
I'm loving and caring.
While waiting for change,
I'm patient, but hurting.
While waiting for change,
My feelings are changing,
My heart is breaking,
I'm fearing and dreading,
Each day that I'm living.
Living with someone,
Who refuses to change,
States, he won't change.
In the midst of my waiting,
For him to change,
A Miscarriage,
Mentally breaking down,
Slowly dying inside,
From stress and disease.
Can't live this painful song,
Tolerated it too long,
I've gotta change,
And move on.

WHILE WAITING FOR CHANGE

<u>INTRODUCTION</u>

"*W*hile Waiting for Change" was written to bring awareness and insight into a very destructive force in society; domestic violence coupled with drug addiction. Many families have suffered and are suffering today because of these dysfunctional issues. It was important for me to write this book and share my experience, in order to help someone else find hope and freedom.

Only some of the traumatizing[1] events in my married life are depicted in this book through poems and chapters.

---

[1] *Trauma-* a very difficult or unpleasant experience that causes someone to have mental or emotional problems usually for a long time "Trauma." Merriam-Webster.com. Accessed January 20, 2016. http://www.merriam-webster.com/dictionary/trauma.

The impact of 20+years of control, manipulation, and all types of abuse, resulted in stress[2] related sicknesses, mental breakdowns and financial problems. The children experienced emotional trauma, causing varying degrees of behavioral and emotional issues. It also affected their focus, attitude and attendance in school.

"While Waiting for Change" is also about relationships. As human beings, we develop some type and level of relationship with people, animals and/or things. Our feelings and emotions often play a role in our decision making, of whom we choose to be a part of our lives. This can cause us to develop relationships with people that are not good/healthy for us. When we hold on to these dysfunctional relationships, (for whatever reason) it brings much distress in our lives and family.

We think we can fix, rescue, change, make people do what's right or what we want them to do, but ultimately it is their choice. Unfortunately, the choices that some people make, cause others to suffer pain and loss.

We all have had varying degrees of traumatic events in our lives. I am sure, there are much

---

[2] *Stress-* A state of mental tension and worry caused by problems in your life, work, etc. person who has been attacked, injured, robbed, or killed by someone else

A person who is cheated or fooled by someone else

Someone or something that is harmed by an unpleasant event (such as an illness or accident) "Stress." Merriam-Webster.com. Accessed January 20, 2016. http://www.merriam-webster.com/dictionary/stress.

worse stories that have or can be told, than mine. Nevertheless, no one should live in an abusive, stress-filled, controlling, manipulative, co-dependent relationship of any degree. Being silent, developing bad habits, becoming co-dependent or an enabler, are not healthy ways to deal with it. Toxic situations like these, can lead to health issues, injury, imprisonment, and/or death.

It is time that we deal with unresolved issues by forgiving people who have hurt us in the present and past, including those in our childhood. Forgiving someone does not mean you allow that person to continue hurting you. Do not get caught in a "forgive, then tolerate more abuse," cycle, like I did. Know when enough is enough for you.

The act of forgiving helps you to release anger and resentment, regain power and control, even after they are physically out of your life. Forgiving takes stress off your mind and body, resulting in clearer thinking, eliminating thoughts of revenge or other foolish, violent actions that bring devastating consequences. You may feel justified in not forgiving, but it is a vital part of moving forward. It is one of the steps in developing healthier relationships, which in turn will create stronger and properly functioning families.

My desire is to encourage and empower someone to make a lifesaving decision, that ends the cycle of a destructive relationship. Please get help! You do not have to become or stay a victim.

***** As you read through the chapters and poems, you may feel like you are reliving an event. I pray that this book will touch, enlighten, strengthen, encourage, move, inspire, and lift you up. God Bless! **********

<u>Note:</u> If you know my ex-husband, please do not look at or treat him like he is a horrible person. He has many good qualities. Unfortunately, while I was married to him, drug addiction played a prominent role in his decision-making. No matter how he treated me, do not get stuck in my story and/or hold anything against him, but show love and forgive. Your relationship with him was different than mine. I have already forgiven him. He expressed to the children how sorry he was for everything. Continue agreeing with me, for his peace, happiness and healing. We all need to be forgiven at some point in our lifetime; none of us are perfect.

*Throughout the book, my thoughts, ideas and opinions, based on my knowledge and experiences, are in italic print, preceded by an asterisk. Please note, what worked for me, may not be the way out for you. All situations are different; everybody's problems cannot be fixed with the same solution. Therefore, I urge everyone to seek professional counseling and sound advice from people who can help you on your journey to freedom safely.

IS THERE ANYBODY OUT THERE?

Is there anybody out there?
Out there for me.
Is there anybody out there?
Who sees me,
Sees that I am good hearted,
Sees that I'm kind,
Sees that I'm beautiful,
Inside and out.
I'm not arrogant or think that I'm it,
But I know God gave me,
Something to give.
Is there anybody out there?
Worthy of the good wife,
That I can be.
Is there anybody out there?
That understands their destiny, my destiny,
And how they intertwine.
Is there any Body?
Some Body?
The Body?
A Body?
That's for me!
I'm tired,
I'm lonely,
Can't wait any longer,
Where is the some-Body for me?

Chapter 1

<u>IN THE BEGINNING...</u>

$\mathcal{I}$ grew up in a house with my mother, father, and two older sisters in Queens, N.Y. My father was a very knowledgeable, wise and proud man. As a handyman by trade, he struggled to provide for us on the salary that he made. Watching him fix things around the house, as a child, taught me how to do simple home repairs as an adult.

My mother was a humble, loving and godly person. She was a Sunday School Primary Class teacher at church and she taught us about God. I also learned how to crochet, knit, cook and sew from my mother.

My sisters and I played in the backyard. We played: dodge ball, "red light, green light, one, two, three," jumped rope and double Dutch, rode bicycles and played in the park. I shared a room with my sister and we had twin beds side by side.

We enjoyed making a tent with our covers draped between the two beds, played with our dolls and read comic books.

My mother took us to church every Sunday. In church, I enjoyed singing in the choir. My sisters and I also sang as a group. We were accompanied by my oldest sister, playing the guitar. At the age of 10, I was asked to sing my first solo in church.

In the midst of all the playing and singing, it was disturbing to hear my father fussing and yelling in the house. I personally thought they were petty issues but apparently he did not feel the same way. For example, he would yell at my mother or complain to anyone that was around, about food in the refrigerator, he thought, should be thrown out. Every time he went into the kitchen, I was afraid for him to open the refrigerator door and look inside.

Things were peaceful, when he was: gardening in the back or front yard, at work, or sitting in the enclosed porch. This is where he looked outside for hours, smoked a cigarette or sang old hymns like "Tis the Old Ship of Zion." I loved hearing him sing. For hours, I sat with my father, watching sports, westerns and old movies on TV. When he started walking around the house, I was hoping that he would not find anything to fuss about.

What troubled me the most in my childhood, is when my father argued with my mother about why he did not want her to go somewhere (especially to church). The arguments about going to church, came as a result of unresolved issues he had with the previous ministry he attended. I can remember my mother's eyes filling up with tears when he said, "No! You can't go today." I felt sad for her, but could not do anything about it.

At the time, I did not know that I was watching a form of verbal/emotional abuse[3] and control playing out, right in front of me. Despite all the wonderful childhood memories, my heart was still troubled and saddened by my mother's emotional pain. Nevertheless, I still loved my father.

When I became a teenager, my interest in being more socially active increased. I had a few friends in school but they were not boys. In church, there were some that I liked but they did not have any interest in me as a girlfriend. In my late teens, there was only one person that I could define as a boyfriend. After that short relationship, I did not date anyone else for years.

The older I became, the desire grew stronger for someone to love and marry me. I wondered when, where, and who was out there for me. Who was going to notice, pay attention and love me? I began to feel undesirable, ugly and rejected. At this point, my self-esteem and confidence was diminishing. A battle started raging inside of me; the emotional and natural needs vs. spiritual truths and holiness.

---

[3] *Abuse-*To treat (a person or animal in a harsh or harmful way to use or treat (something in a way that causes damage to use (something) wrongly "Abuse." Merriam-Webster.com. Accessed January 20, 2016. http://www.merriamwebster.com/dictionary/abuse

As I looked for love and companionship, loneliness became the driving force.

I really did not know who I was or how to love myself. When I was appointed to be the church Youth Leader, I thought, "How can I help these people, when I need help myself?" But to keep from focusing on being lonely, I stayed busy in ministry. I knew God, my family, and church family loved me, but that was not enough. I just could not wait any longer.

Have you ever felt lonely in a house filled with people? When overwhelmed with loneliness, vulnerability[4] increases, causing us to connect with anyone that shows interest in us.

Ignoring personal issues and core problems by staying busy, will not make them disappear. Dealing with/resolving them, helps to reduce our emotional instability and vulnerability. I believe that it is important to: love God and ourselves, know who we are, be honest with ourselves about what we want out of life, confront our thoughts and emotions and how we feel/should feel about them. All these things, can help us make sound decisions about relationships and our future.

Prayerfully consider every prophetic word and/ or an opinion about who your mate should be,

---

[4] *Vulnerable*-easily hurt or harmed physically, mentally, or emotionally Open to attack, harm, or damage "Vulnerable." Merriam-Webster. com. Accessed January 20, 2016. http://www.merriam-webster.com/ dictionary/vulnerable

especially if you are lonely. If it is accurate, wait for the right time, making sure that you are able to handle a relationship/marriage emotionally and financially. Hasty decisions/commitments can turn into bondage/prison sentences that you may not be able to get out of, until someone is hurt or dies.

TO THE RESCUE

Thought I was doing something good,
Saw someone hurting and thought I could,
Help!
I felt confident in my faith and ability,
To get through the darkness of addiction,
So he would be set free.
Didn't realize the details,
And what depths I was committing to,
I just wanted to *fix* him,
Maybe he would also love me and say "I do."

Chapter 2

MEETING MY HUSBAND TO BE

As a teenager in the 70s, I met the cousins of my "not yet" husband, while going to different church services in New York City. My sisters and I would hang out with them often because we really enjoyed their company. Several months later, I met him after his mother became a member of our church. He was a year older than I, doing "his thing" in the streets. On the rare occasion that he came to church, he never paid any attention to me.

Over a decade went by before I saw him again. I was now a junior missionary in another ministry. His uncle, the pastor of a church in Brooklyn, asked if I would sing a solo at a revival service and I consented. My "not yet" husband was there with his mother and father. After the service, they drove me home. He and I started talking about the past and other things, then about God and the Bible.

At this time in my life, I was drained from "church busyness" and had not dealt with personal issues and feelings. My flesh and emotions were stronger than the spiritual part of me. As I was speaking and looking at him, I could feel my body and emotions, reaching out for a response from him. They seemed to be, pulling on and out of him what I needed and wanted for my flesh. At that point, I was not focused on ministering to him as a soul. I still tried to talk to him about God, but I was deceived to think that I was spiritually strong enough to handle it.

His parents were planning their move to Florida to retire. I spoke to his mother to find out what was going on with him. She gave me details of his struggle with drugs and her concern about him staying in the city when they left.

I felt, as a missionary, that I could help him get over his addiction[5] and they would not have to worry about him when they left. I made time to meet with him again, thinking and trying to convince myself that we were only going to discuss the Bible and pray. But I am also hoping that he has an interest in me, thinking that once he became a Christian (saved), he would be "the one."

---

[5] *Addiction*-noun: a strong and harmful need to regularly have something (such as a drug) or do something (such as gamble) an unusually great interest in something or a need to do or have something "Addiction." Merriam-Webster.com. Accessed January 20, 2016. http://www.merriamwebster.com/dictionary/addiction

ç*He was an addict[6] and I had no idea about that way of life. Have you ever had good intentions, but your flesh and emotions took over? When the relationship does not work, you wish you never got involved with the person.

I was so naïve about drug addiction and street life that I did not know what I was getting myself into. His world was entirely different from the church environment I grew up in. I was now his rescuer and protector. Despite his drug use I still wanted to marry him.

---

[6] *Addict-* a person who is not able to stop taking drugs a person who is addicted to drugs a person who likes or enjoys something very much and spends a large amount of time doing it, watching it, etc.
transitive verb of addict- 1: to devote or surrender (oneself) to something habitually or obsessively<addicted to gambling> 2: to cause addiction to a substance in (a person or animal)"Addict." Merriam-Webster.com. Accessed January 20, 2016. http://www.merriam-webster.com/dictionary/addict.

DON'T DO IT!

If you are lonely,
Don't do it!
If you're filling a void in you,
Don't do it!
If you are weak and confused,
Don't do it!
If you are emotionally drained,
Don't do it!
If you can't swim,
Please! Don't do it!
Don't get involved and go to their rescue,
Their sea of problems and emotions,
Just may be too deep for you.
In their hurt and pain,
You'll begin to sink.
Finding yourself drowning too,
Who will be there to rescue you?

*Thinking we know someone, is not enough! Whoever you meet, try to find out from them and/or others (family, friends, thorough background check, etc...), about their past. Both of you must know the motives, intents, agendas and expectations of the relationship. Are you both expecting more out of each other than can be given? Are you ignoring negative behaviors, because of their attractiveness? Do they have anything of value to offer? What about their character and integrity?

Find out if you are compatible in all areas (likes, dislikes, religious beliefs, having and raising children, etc.). With the information you gather, make a wise choice on what to do. What type and level of relationship should you have with them? Maybe you shouldn't have a relationship with them at all.

Please get counseling from someone who will impart wisdom to you and your potential spouse. Proceed with great caution! You can have a heavenly marriage or a marital nightmare.

LOSING ME

Lost in your world,
Your thoughts are becoming my thoughts,
Where you went, I went in my mind.
Everyday!
I did what you wanted me to do,
In your way.
Who am I?
Am I you?
Your angry voice in my head,
Seeing or hearing you,
I would dread.
Who am I?
Am I you?
Where am I?
I'm lost in you,
And your world of insanity.
What happened to *MY* dreams?
Were they just a lie?
Did they die?
Is my future you?
I'm losing me!
What do I do?

Chapter 3

HIS WORLD

*It's interesting how we think a person will fit into our world. We believe we are in control and have ideas of how people will relate to us in our environment. They come, however, with their own world views, values, perceptions and perhaps misconceptions of you and your world.

Some people you allow in your world, want to/ will control you with their belief systems, ideas, and philosophies. Now, your world does not exist, it is all about them; what they want, what they expect of you, and how you will be in their world.

If someone is intimidated by your accomplishments and does not: let you be you, support your dreams, encourage and/or work with you, then please beware. There is a great possibility, they will belittle, discourage, control and manipulate you.

*****The two worlds should become as, "one syn-chronized, harmonious symphony of love," as you both work to build a future together.******
(This does not mean that you will not
have any disagreements)

The dysfunctional relationship started before the marriage. When he asked for money I gave it to him, knowing he was going to use it for drugs. Despite all the flashing warning signs and loud sirens going off all around me, I refused to accept the truth. Family and church friends advised me not to get involved with him but I did not listen. Loneliness blinded and deafened me to the truth. If I acknowledged and accepted the truth, I would have to let go of someone who *I* thought, would fill the void in my life.

I hoped he wanted me as much as I wanted him. However, neither one of us was emotionally, mentally or financially stable to have a serious relationship. I needed him to replace feelings of loneliness, rejection, and neglect; it seemed like he only needed me to finance his drug habit.

I consented to live in his world, not knowing it was filled with pain, hurt and rejection from his past. He turned to crack cocaine for medication in order to dull the painful feelings. Unfortunately, it did not fix his issues but only created more problems. His addictive behaviors created a world of: instability, depression, poverty, manipulation, lies, stealing, selfishness, blaming, denial, and pure insanity. It was like poison, affecting his heart, crippling his mind and the ability to express true love or be consistent in understanding and caring.

I stepped into his world, thinking I could rescue him out of this world. When I married him, I went even deeper into this dark world that I knew nothing about. I said I do, but to WHAT? Now I am drowning, drowning in his world of addiction to crack cocaine. *Who* is going to rescue me?

WHO'S GONNA RESCUE YOU?

Who's gonna rescue you?
When you can no longer breathe!
Drowning in a sea of emotions,
Deceptive thinking and fear,
Will someone hear, Your cry?
Or will they just pass you by?
Who's gonna see?
When you're struggling to get free.
Well,
YOUR RESCUER IS COMING!
God Sent,
A person, a message or just one word.
You may be snatched out,
Or you may have to run!
Don't miss your time and opportunity,
When it comes,
It may be your only one!

WRECKLESS DRIVER

Why did I give you control over me?
When you had no control over yourself.
Handling me like a reckless driver,
Driving me down dark roads,
To nowhere.
Turning me into dark alleys,
And parking me there,
To be stripped and vandalized,
Broken windows and dented sides.
Shifting me in and out of gears,
Of trust and mistrust,
Love and hate,
Joy and sadness.
Stepping over limits and boundaries,
By running red lights and stop signs.
Causing lapses in insurance and inspections,
By not taking care of me and keeping me covered.
Jerking motions,
Stopping and starting,
You've worn down the brakes.
You're out of control!
Look out!
Stop!
We've crashed and burned,
The relationship is totaled!

Chapter 4

MARRIED TO HIS WORLD

Now as his wife, I am still looking for the love, security, provider, and friend that I wanted. I found out the hard way; he was incapable of being that kind of husband.

Where is the love? What is his definition of love? Everyone has their own perception, definition, and philosophy about love, cultivated through their own experiences with family, friends and religious groups/churches.

My husband was incapable of covering, protecting or been totally committed to me. Apparently, he was already married to an illegal drug. It was like I was in a polygamous relationship. He cared more for the drug than he did for me. He chased the drug, lied for the drug, stole for the drug, manipulated for the drug, was sex driven by the drug, went to bed thinking about the drug and woke up thinking about how to get more of the drug. I should not have said, "I do" to this.

Traditionally, the father gives consent to the man to marry the daughter. During the ceremony it is asked, "Who gives this woman to this man?" The father replies "I do." Recently, God gave me this revelation; God said that He did not give me to this man (especially in the state that he was in), nor His blessing or consent to marry him. He just honored His covenant of marriage. I made the choice and I said "I do."

God, as our heavenly Father does not always approve of whom we want to marry. Sometimes we move too fast and agree to things, without the blessing of the Father. We just have to have that man/woman. We just have to get married. You both may be thinking; if we are burning with desire then we might as well get married. Well, I tell you, some marriages become a type of hell and you will still find yourself burning, but painfully so. The pain and heartache we are experiencing, replaces our original thoughts of how beautiful the marriage would, could or should be.

You may start thinking, "Why did I want this so bad?" "Why didn't I/why couldn't I wait?" It will not matter how much you spent on the wedding, how beautiful you looked or how beautiful the wedding was, you will be wishing it never happened.

In the beginning of the marriage, we lived with his parents for a very short time before they moved to Florida. We then moved into my mother's house, but he began to steal things and sell them for drugs. We could not stay there or anywhere for long, because of his addictive behaviors. Sometimes when he used drugs, he stayed out for days. I looked out the window day and night; worried, praying constantly, waiting for him to come home. He eventually got caught with drugs and went to jail.

After praying, I should not have worried, but taking on the role of his rescuer and protector, I was not able to leave him in God's hands. Fear, stress and worry are now affecting my body and mind. Sicknesses, diseases and disorders were developing and they eventually manifested.

In the prison he went to, they had a place where married couples could spend a weekend together (conjugal visits), periodically. During the visit, I became pregnant with our first child. We were both excited about it and I was hoping the thought of becoming a father, would make him stop using drugs.

I was happy to give birth to a healthy baby boy, but upset because I married out of the will of God and that his father was in prison. This was not how I wanted my marriage or family to start. I did not feel God loved or forgave me and it was hard to forgive myself. While sitting in my mother's room, I watched Kenneth Copeland, minister the word of God. He pointed to the camera and said, "God still loves you." The tears began to flow down my face, I knew that message was for me. The weight of guilt lifted off my heart. I believed I was loved and forgiven by God. It was at that moment, I forgave myself.

When my husband returned from prison, my mother allowed him to stay at the house. I was happy, he finally could see his son. Not too long after, he began to steal and cause trouble again so she told *him* to leave. Now he is out on the streets; I am hoping he would go into a rehab, but he didn't. A couple of days passed before he contacted me, asking if I would bring him something to eat.

The next time he came to the front door, I was holding our son in my arms. As soon as I opened the door, he reached out to his father and started crying. When I saw the look in my husband's eyes and the expression on his face, my heart sank. I just could not keep his son away from him any longer. I felt it was time for us to be together like a real family. At that point, I decided to go into a shelter.

I'm thinking; Now we have a child and he still has not changed. Why didn't he get himself together in jail? Why do I still have to go through this and now, into a shelter?

THE COST IS TOO HIGH

Paid my time, money and energy,
For you!
Sacrificed my health,
And my sanity too,
But was that enough, enough for you?
Sacrificed the children's well-being,
My identity too,
Shouldn't that be enough,
Enough for you?
The cost is *too* high to be with you!

------*So as I walk away*------

I have,
No money,
No time,
No energy,
No explanation,
No anything.
I just can't be with *YOU*,
Your cost is too high,
I'm through!

Chapter 5

<u>THE COST IS TOO HIGH</u>

My husband's addictive behaviors, caused him to continuously take all types of finances from the household. In addition to taking cash, he sold: paper food stamps, W.I.C (women, infant, children) food/infant formula vouchers, diapers, food, clothes, and much more for the "high." His drug use kept us in poverty. Going into a shelter because of it, just added to the nightmare.

The first shelter we went to had an infestation of roaches, flying water bugs and mice. I sprayed until I got rid of those disgusting bugs and stuffed a cloth under the door to stop the mice from running in and out. I made the shelter in to our temporary home, just for the sake of being a family.

I remember, as I began to wash dishes; the tears ran down my face. I cried out to God asking Him, "When will this be over?" He said to me, "In the midst of your mess, I will fix it." God did not tell me how and when, but after hearing those words, I wiped the tears from my eyes and finished washing the dishes. It gave me a sense of hope and assurance that eventually, things were going to change.

Now pregnant with our second son, nearing the time of delivery, there was an argument between my husband and the shelter security guard. Still trying to be the rescuer and protector, I stepped in between them as they were about to fight. I started pushing on them, screaming and yelling for them to stop. It was a crazy thing to do, but they stopped. Feeling dizzy and breathing hard now, the shelter staff called for someone to take my blood pressure. Needless to say, it was very high. They had me relax in the office until it was normal, then I went to my room. After our son was born, they transferred us to a shelter in the Bronx.

Where ever we went I had to find a church in the area, for that extra spiritual support in order to function during the week. We did not have a car nor did I have money for us to get on the bus. Everywhere we went we had to walk. Since my sons were still young I needed a stroller to take them with me. I was blessed with a used stroller and we were now rolling all over the place.

I was pushing that hand-me-down stroller; uptown, downtown, across town, to get to food pantries and find clothes for the children. The plastic frame on the wheels cracked under the weight of children, food and other things. I had to find something to hold the wheels together, to get my children and everything else home. When I got to the house, I took string and duct tape, to fix the wheels. It kept us rolling, until we were given another stroller.

We finally moved into our own apartment in Brooklyn. Through a community agency, we were able to get new bunk beds for the children and other furniture. Not too long after, my husband went back to jail for drug possession. When he came home, he was still out of control.

The need for crack cocaine continuously drove my husband out into the streets. It had him finding ways to get it at any cost. Fear and dread came upon me, whenever he entered the house, after getting "high." I knew he was going to take something out of the house to sell. But this one particular time, the feeling was different and stronger than usual. Something real crazy was about to happen.

I cannot remember how the conversation started, but he said he was taking the furniture. We argued about it, but he had already found someone with a truck to take the bunk beds and everything else. So the children and I left the house. I did not want them to watch the furniture go out the front door, neither could I stand to see it happen. When we came back, it was all gone. I packed some clothes and we went to my mother's house. Meanwhile, my husband was getting "high" and we were homeless again.

I made phone calls at my mother's house, to find another shelter. There was an opening for us in the Bronx. The next day, my husband met me in Queens and before getting on the train to go the shelter, we got help with food and money. After packing our clothes in a black garbage bag, some food and other necessities in a large duffel bag, we were on our way.

As we were traveling through Manhattan towards Harlem, I began to see those familiar signs of him wanting to use drugs; the fear and dread hit me. I knew he was going to get off the train. He was looking around, getting very fidgety, then asked for the money and took the frozen packaged meat out of the large duffel bag. He got off the train in Harlem.

There was a woman watching and hearing our conversation and saw him get off the train. When we arrived at our stop in the Bronx, she offered to help me with the bags and the children. She took us to a store to get whatever we needed; called a taxi and went with us to the shelter. She stayed with us until the completion of the intake process; put some money in my hand and said goodbye. I believe she was truly an angel sent from God to help me.

I pleaded for him to stop and hoped that the love (I thought he had) for me and the children would make him change. However, the drug had a strong grip on his will. He continued using but I am waiting for change.

Although people and agencies came to help us, things could have been better. This was not the way I grew up. Never thought, in my wildest nightmares, I would be living like this. I began to feel the guilt and regret of tolerating the insanity. The children became victims[7] of his drug addicted and abusive behaviors which affected them emotionally and mentally. The cost was too high for this madness to continue.

---

[7]   _Victim-_a person who has been attacked, injured, robbed, or killed by someone else a person who is cheated or fooled by someone else someone or something that is harmed by an unpleasant event (such as an illness or accident) "Victim." Merriam-Webster.com. Accessed January 20, 2016. http://www.merriam-webster.com/dictionary/victim.

NO MORE

Flooded by emotions,
Crippled by fear,
Can't move,
Can't breathe,
Can't think,
No more!
Pain rushes to my head,
Brain shuts down,
Helplessness grips me,
I have no control.
I say,
NO MORE!
I break your hold,
And the cycle of control.
Leave my space,
Leave my mind,
It's over, it's done,
Covenant already broken!
You can't come back,
Won't let you back,
No More, No more, No more!
No more, will I let you hurt me!
No more, will I let you take control,
No more, will you take advantage of me!
No more, No more, No more!
But……..

Chapter 6

CAN'T DO THIS NO MORE!

We were transferred from the Bronx into a Brooklyn shelter. I am now pregnant with our first daughter and waiting to move into an apartment. A few months after moving in, she was born.

We became members of a church in Brooklyn, where God began to strengthen me. I started working in the ministry and singing in the choir. My husband also joined the choir and made friends with many of the men in the church. They took him out on jobs with them to make money, but it just went up in "drug smoke." He just was not ready to stop.

A few years later, when I was about to begin a new missionary/ministers training class, things turned for the worse. He was now owing drug dealers. While my husband went to use drugs; he sent me to pay them with paper food stamps and money. It was now getting dangerous; fear, stress, worry, nervousness and anxiety was increasing. My husband did not seem to care if our lives were in danger.

There are many women who find themselves and their children in danger, dealing with these types of situations.

While pregnant with our last child (another girl), after he came home from using drugs, I asked him, "What do you value, your family or drugs?" He turned his head, as he laid in the bed, grumbling something I did not understand and went to sleep. However, his answer was clear, by what he continued to do. I pleaded with God to get me out of this. All of these questions began flooding my mind: *Why did I do this to myself in the first place? "God, what do you want me to do now?" Should I leave? How do I leave? When do I leave? Where do I go and how will I get there? Who's going to help me? Who do I tell? What do I tell them? What do I do after I leave?*

Prior to leaving, I told him that it was the last month I was doing this, but he still did not pay any attention to me. The next time I received cash assistance and food stamps, I planned to pay off the drug dealer, wait for my husband to leave on his mission, then take the children and go.

A few days before leaving, I made arrangements to meet my mother at the home of the person, she helped throughout the week. When that day came, I did just what I planned. After paying off the drug dealer, I had no cash, only $97 worth of food stamps, for me (now six months pregnant) and our three children. I took one big black garbage bag and filled it with our clothes. All our important papers were put into another bag and the children's backpacks were filled with some of their things.

I hurried up and got the kids out of there; scared, looking around, hoping not to run into him, as we made our way to the bus stop. When we arrived at the person's house, I immediately called the Domestic Violence Hotline. They connected me to a domestic violence shelter in Albany. The Pastor of my church, provided the money for the bus trip and we left late that afternoon.

By now, you may be saying: "She was crazy for letting him do that to her and the children" and/or "If that was me, I would have never stayed that long," or a whole lot of other things. Unfortunately, some people, when they realize what is happening to them, they feel trapped, hoping that it will work out, and/ or too afraid to leave or fight back.

I thought I could fix a bad situation to fit my thought and perception of what the relationship should be. I held on to hope because of the good I saw in him. But when it turned ugly again, I wanted to let go. I began to feel like I was living with "Dr. Jekyll and Mr. Hyde."

POWER SHIFTS

Taken by control,
Power to say "no",
Stripped from my tongue!
Powerless to resist,
Threatened into giving in,
Gripped by fear,
No Power to let go.

-----*Power Shift!*-----

Caught a glimpse of freedom,
Felt empowered by God,
The power to say "No!"
I'm taking back control!
Power to resist!
The enemy has to flee!
Power to stand tall!
Power to face it all!
Power to let go!
So Why! Do I
Allow!
Another Power Shift?

Chapter 7

POWER SHIFTS

When we arrived upstate, we were back in the shelter system again. I did not know anyone or how to get around in the community. Now I am facing a new environment; pregnant with three children, alone.

I asked the residents in the shelter, how to get to the elementary school, to enroll the two oldest children in first grade and kindergarten. On school days, I took all three children on two buses, along with my pregnant belly, from the shelter to the school and back. In the midst of this strange place, with pregnancy hormones acting up and no family or friends, my mind and emotions were going crazy. Thank God, for His strength, mercy, kindness, and faithfulness that met me every morning, to take me through the day.

I contacted my mother to let her know that we arrived upstate safely, but never told her the name of the city, we were in. I asked her not to tell my husband, when he calls. When he finally came back to the house, a few hours passed before he realized we left. He immediately called my mother, but she did not tell him that we were upstate. By the end of that month, he had to leave the apartment because he could not take care of the bills.

I called my mother to find out what was going on with him and the apartment. She told me that he went to a rehab facility in Albany. When I heard that, my heart sank, I felt weak and sick to my stomach. It seemed like I just could not get away from him. I let my mother know that I was in Albany also (don't remember her reaction). I told her that she and the neighbors could take whatever they wanted out of the apartment, and then give the keys to the landlord.

My husband is now in the same city that we are in. Even though, he did not know that we were there, I was still afraid. I asked my caseworker at the shelter to move us somewhere else. She named a few places, but I did not ask how far they were from Albany. Around that time, our youngest son developed chicken pox. They would not let us transfer to anywhere, until he was cleared by a doctor. So as soon as the untimely chicken pox episode was over, we were moved to the YWCA in Schenectady. I did not realize it was less than 20 minutes away from Albany.

We stayed in their domestic violence shelter for about two months, before moving into our new apartment. Our youngest daughter was born two months after we moved in. The real estate agent offered to help furnish the apartment. She spoke to her family members and friends and they came with two truckloads of furniture. All I could do was cry and say thank you. Just as I gave away all I had in my apartment in Brooklyn to others, the Lord gave it back to me through others in upstate New York. She also spoke to her co-workers and they blessed me with money and things for the baby. Other people I met during the transition process, connected me to more resources.

I was finally settling into this new environment. I had control over my finances and we were able to get and keep things. The children seemed happy. They enjoyed playing in the backyard and I had a lot of fun watching children's movies with them. I also found another church and became a member. They were a great support to me and the children.

Three months after our daughter was born, I heard that my husband was doing well. I wanted him to see his new baby girl. Since my mother's church was having a special birthday celebration service for her in New York City, I thought it would be safe for him to see us there. So he came to the birthday celebration. He looked physically well, seemed mentally OK, and was happy to see us. I still was not ready to let him know where we were living.

Three months after seeing him in New York City, we started speaking to each other on a regular basis. He said a lot of good and convincing things that made me believe he changed. But I was emotionally blinded to the real truth because of my strong desire to be together as a family. Thinking and hoping he

49

was finally ready to take care of us, I let him back into our lives. He was very helpful around the house: he cooked (great cook), cleaned, made the bed and ironed his clothes. He made sure the children did chores. He was loving, caring and kind. I enjoyed this glimpse of hope and change. Unfortunately, the addictive behaviors were not totally under control, as he portrayed.

My husband started looking for jobs and was hired, but could not keep them very long. As soon as he got his paycheck he wasted it on crack cocaine. He was still under the control of the old addictive patterns and behaviors. He started making excuses for his behavior, saying, "I've been doing this all my life." Even after my husband said that, it was hard for me to believe that he did not want to change.

I really loved him, and on occasion, I felt he loved me. But it was like the other wife (drugs) kept calling him and driving him to leave, hate, threaten, neglect, abuse and abandon me and the children. It wanted all of his time and attention.

Well, *here we go again*! The power is shifting out of my hands, back into his. Why was I letting this happen again? Do I really want to put myself and our children through the insanity again, while I wait for him to change?

I'M THINKING

I'm thinking,
If I act a certain way,
If I continue to fast and pray,
If I keep the faith,
Then maybe, he'll change.
I'm thinking,
If I'm feeling sick and hospitalized,
He'll stop and realize,
Maybe,
Just maybe, he'll change.
If I call the police,
To stop the insanity,
He will have no other choice,
But to change.
I'm thinking,
I'll do what he says,
Give him what he wants,
Then he will change.
I'm thinking,
Don't defend the children,
When he goes after them,
He gets angry when I do,
Yeah!
That's what I'll do.
But, I came to realize,
What I was thinking,
He was not.
Only thinking of himself,
And, no one else.

So NOW,
I'm thinking,
It's time for *ME* to *change*!
Think about me,
And the children's safety,
Let go and move on,
It's time to be free!

Chapter 8

<u>WHAT WILL IT TAKE FOR CHANGE?</u>

Not understanding what I was up against, I wondered what has to happen for him to change.

At the end of the delivery of my last child, the doctor told me I had too many fibroids in my uterus and it would not be wise to go through another pregnancy. So within a few months, after a lot of pain, I had some tests done. They not only saw the fibroids, but they found cysts on my ovaries and pre-cervical cancer. They suggested that I have a total hysterectomy and get rid of everything (no more baby making factory). The surgery caused me to go into "surgical menopause" (no more menstrual cycle, *Yeah, I thought*). This brought on the hot flashes and the other menopausal symptoms that I did not enjoy.

They offered me estrogen pills to counteract the effects of menopause. But when they informed me that the risk of developing breast cancer would increase, I told them, "No." My grandmother had breast cancer and eventually died after it spread to other parts of her body. My mother was recovering from breast cancer during this time. I did not want to take the risk. My husband was a great help to me during my recovery, after the hysterectomy surgery. But eventually, he relapsed into an active addiction pattern again.

After recovering from the operation, I volunteered my time to the outreach ministries at church: food pantry, clothing room and soup kitchen. As I regained my strength I started looking for a job and was hired at McDonalds. Now that my husband was using again, the stress and worry began increasing.

Only after a month of working, I began feeling tired, dizzy and nauseous every day. After several weeks of feeling this way, while I was working, I felt a dull pain in my right breast. When I touched the area, I felt a lump the size of a nickel. I finished my shift; left the job thinking about the lump in my breast, knowing I had to get it checked out.

I immediately made an appointment to see a doctor. Upon examining me, the doctor sent me for a mammogram. After seeing the results of the test, he informed me that they needed to take a biopsy of the lump, because it could possibly be cancerous.

After the hysterectomy, I refused to take the estrogen pills so I would not increase my chances of developing breast cancer. Now I am facing it anyway.

The results of the biopsy came back positive for cancer. They sent me to a surgeon, who gave me more information about the tumor and the options that I had to get rid of it. He asked, "How many children do you have and how old are they?" I got choked up and started crying, when I began to tell him their age because they were so young; my oldest son was eight and my youngest daughter was only 18 months old.

As the tears flowed, I turned my face away from him and said (in my mind) "Lord, please let me live to see my children grow up." I felt like the biblical character, Hezekiah, when he turned his face to the wall and asked God to spare his life, after he received the bad news about his health.

After the operation I was sent to an oncologist. I went through chemotherapy treatment for about five months. All my hair fell out so I wore wigs. The majority of the time I felt tired and weak, never vomited or lost weight, but started gaining weight (that was a surprise).

Because of the drug use, my husband was not there for his family emotionally, physically, or financially. However, God took care and provided for us through the entire ordeal. Many people came with cooked meals and helped take care of the children, while I recuperated.

The oncologist told me, she would not be surprised if it returned within two years after treatment because of the type of cancer I had. But thank God, I am still cancer free! He has granted me to see; my sons and oldest daughter graduate from high school and my first grandchild. I am expecting to live and enjoy the good things God has planned for my life.

After recovering from breast cancer, I worked one year as a volunteer through the Americorps Literacy Program, in an elementary school. Immediately after the assignment was over, I was hired as an assistant teacher's aide in a day care center.

I wanted to go into the Human Services field in order to help others. So I enrolled in the Bachelor's degree program at Empire State College. I received financial aid and registered for online courses so I did not have to travel to the college. Despite the stress around me, God blessed me to do very well in all the courses.

When my husband found out that I was getting a refund from financial aid (after tuition and books) he demanded some of the money to buy drugs. I was not able to get what I really wanted for me or the children because of this. After I did all the work, it just wasn't fair for him to have any of it but I was too weak and afraid to enforce my "No." I wanted to stop completely for that reason, but I still continued.

Eventually, the family issues became too much for me to concentrate on college work. I changed my degree plan to an Associates and obtained an A.S. degree in Human Services. It was disheartening for me to do this because I was only 24 credits away

from receiving a BA degree in Human Services/
Counseling.

*Abusers can sabotage your dreams, if you let them.
It is hard to stay focused on what YOU want to do
or be. All your focus turns to their issues and needs.*

BREATHE

Each pay day,
I held my breath,
On the job,
Waiting,
Feeling the stress.
The phone rings,
What will he say?
How much will it be?
When I can't afford anything.
Thinking,
This time I'll stand up for myself,
I won't go through with it,
I'll just say "No!"
But my "No" means nothing,
I still have to do it.
Emotionally stressed,
When can I take a breath?
The same thing happens,
Time after time,
Tell me, when will everything be fine?
Come on now!
I'm about to suffocate,
Can't hold it any longer.
Lack of oxygen,
My heart is under attack,
I've got to breathe,
Breathe, Breathe,
Inhale, exhale,
Heart gotta start pumping again.

I need help,
Gotta stand up for myself,
I can't die here,
Gotta get out of here,
I've got to Breathe!

Chapter 9

<u>CAN I BREATHE?</u>

While I was working at the daycare center, he called frequently. It became embarrassing and I was told by the receptionist and supervisor that there were too many calls coming in for me. Going to work was my place of escape from the madness, but I still could not get any peace.

At the beginning of every pay week, the stress and fear of what he was going to do and ask for, caused my stomach to hurt. My husband had already decided how much he wanted out of the check for drugs. We argued about the money the night before, and sometimes in the store. If I did not give him what he wanted, he threatened to take more or all of it. A half hour before I left the job, he was on his way to the check cashing place to wait for me. I just dreaded this day so much.

This made it hard to pay the bills and the rent, but it seemed like he didn't care and I understood why (the drug). My husband did not take responsibility for any of the important bills. When he had a job, he rented electronics from Aarons or Rent-a-Center, made a few payments and then lost job because of drugs.

The drug addictive behaviors were choking the life out of our family and finances. How long did I have to inhale/hold my breath before things changed? When could I come up for air and breathe/exhale, emotionally and financially?

When the children grew older, their video games and the valuable things that they loved were sold for drugs. They would cry and get angry, asking why was their father doing this to them. The older they got, the harder it was for them to handle the loss of what was taken. They could not understand how could someone love them and sell their things for drugs. It was painful for me to see them hurting. I did not realize the long-term effect it would have on them. None of us could breathe a sigh of relief; we never knew when and what was going to be taken next. All of us were suffocating from everything going up in "drug smoke."

We suffered, while he was out getting "high," furnishing the drug dealers' homes, and paying their bills, with the money and things that belonged to his family. He would find a way to replace the items, but not too long after, they would be gone again. This created a vicious and stressful cycle of insanity. I often wondered, how did he feel about what he was doing to us.

Comforting them with some kind of explanation, was not good enough; their anger and frustration just increased. I talked to my husband about how the children felt.

He apologized to us after the episodes. Unfortunately, the repeated incidents made the apologies seem void. I was afraid that the children would eventually lash out at him, causing someone to get hurt. These stressful situations were wearing on my heart, mind and body. I felt like a single mom with a marriage license, living with a thief who had a key.

Children can take but so much before they snap and they should not be pushed to that point. Ephesians 6:4 in the Amplified Version states, *"Fathers, do not provoke your children to anger (do not exasperate[8] them to the point of resentment with demands that are trivial or unreasonable or humiliating or abusive; nor by showing favoritism or indifference to any of them), but bring them up (tenderly, with lovingkindness) in the discipline and instruction of the Lord."[9]*

---

[8] Exasperate: to make (someone) very angry or annoyed "Exasperate." Merriam-Webster.com. Accessed January 28, 2016. http://www.merriam-webster.com/dictionary/exasperate.

[9] Scripture quotations taken from the Amplified® Bible, Copyright © 2015 by The Lockman Foundation. Used by permission." (www.Lockman.org

*If you have children in the house, the dysfunc-
tional behavior will definitely affect and infect them.
It will show up, sooner and later in their adult years.
I'm speaking from what I see them going through
now. There is no easy, nor quick fix for the years of
trauma they experienced. We pay for our choices
and unfortunately, others pay for them, as well.*

ENABLER

Sacrificing myself,
My children,
Our well-being.
Trapped,
Afraid to say,
"No"
Choices, will and identity,
All taken away.
YOUR will is being done,
YOUR needs are being met,
Over ours!
Covering and taking up for you,
But we're not covered.
I'm protecting you,
But, who's protecting us?

Chapter 10

THE ENABLER'S PRISON

I enabled[10] my husband to continue using and abusing by: protecting, intervening, making excuses for his behavior, giving him money and paying off bills he created. I did not allow him to take responsibility for his actions.

Whatever my husband asked for, I found some way to get it. I had to make sure he was "happy" 24/7 or there would be no peace in the house. The children's needs were sacrificed in order to take care of their father. They were being neglected, financially and paternally.

---

[10] *Enabler-*one that enables another to achieve an end; especially: one who enables another to persist in self-destructive behavior (as substance abuse) by providing excuses or by making it possible to avoid the consequences of such behavior "Enabler." Merriam-Webster. com. Accessed January 20, 2016. http://www.merriam-webster.com/dictionary/enabler

Doing everything my husband demanded, was very stressful. I continued feeling pain in my stomach. The effects of fear, worry and nervousness was, unknowingly causing damage to the lining in my stomach. One day I started coughing up blood. I went to the emergency room and after running tests, they found that the lining of my stomach was bleeding. They diagnosed me with Gastritis; I knew it was stress related. The pain continued to bother my stomach every time there was an episode of him using drugs.

Desperate for the madness to stop, I had to do something, but what? I was too afraid to talk to anyone or stand up to my husband for fear of being hurt. Time in prisons and rehab facilities did not change or stop him. This enabling relationship had to end.

Being an enabler is not just a crutch to the other person, but it empowers them to take advantage of you. They turn you into their puppet, victim and prisoner. In order to keep some type of peace in the house, you try to do everything the abuser says. When you refuse to do it, they threaten and/or use other types of abuse to keep you under submission. This is not peace, but oppression, control, and manipulation; restricting you from getting what is needed/wanted for yourself and children.

IMPRISONED

I'm imprisoned in my home and my mind,
Locked in by hopes and dreams,
Believing that you'll change,
And there will be better days.
Doing the same thing,
Every day, the same way.
I'm held hostage by the thoughts,
That it's all my fault.
Could'ves, would'ves and should'ves,
Torment me, as I wait,
Behind these bars.
I'm losing my health,
My mind, my children and myself.
My faith is shaking,
Now I'm breaking,
Believing there is no escaping.
Is this a life sentence?
When will I be released?
Where's the guard with the key?
Telling me,
Time to leave, You're free!

*Why did I allow his addictive behavior to continue affecting the family? Is this a life sentence? I'm thinking about how I got out before, but things are different now. I cannot keep relocating; how long will it take for deliverance to come this time?

He eventually was caught with drugs and went to jail again. I thought about taking this opportunity to tell him it was over, but I was not strong enough (yet). Fear, religious beliefs and my thoughts kept me in the marriage. I felt stuck and imprisoned, still waiting for things to change.

A few years later, I was introduced to an awesome, wise woman of God who pastored a church in Albany. After visiting a few times, the entire family joined the church.

My husband enjoyed the services. On Sundays, he loved to dress in suits. He looked sharp from head to toe. If he did not starch and iron his shirts, he brought them to the cleaners to have them laundered and starched. I was hoping, he would finally get delivered from drugs. However, it was still his choice, to yield to the process of change. I'm thinking, at least he's going to church.

I felt connected to the ministry and was empowered by the teachings. The woman of God, counselled and encouraged me to be strong. She prayed fervently for me and my family. I finally had someone to talk to.

CAN'T LIVE LIKE THIS

Feeling suicidal,
Can't live like this no more.
Feeling suicidal,
I just can't tell no one.
Feeling suicidal,
Wish my life was done.
Feeling suicidal,
Why suffer any more pain?
Feeling suicidal,
Unless my sanity, I can regain.
Feeling suicidal,
Is there hope for me?
Feeling suicidal,
I just want to be free!
Feeling suicidal,
Some things I didn't choose.
Feeling suicidal,
What do I have to lose?
Feeling suicidal,
Is there another way out, to be free?
Free from pain,
Free from hurting,
Free from tears,
Free from stress,
Free from struggling,
Free from straining,
Pressure, control and bondage.
Who can I trust to tell this all to?
I'm crying out!...Can I get HELP from *You*?

Why doesn't anyone notice?
Can't anyone see?
Is it hidden that well inside of me?
But Now, it's time!
I want to Live and Live free!
Can't live like this!
HELP, HELP, PLEASE HELP ME!

Chapter 11

DON'T WANT TO *LIVE* LIKE THIS!

$\mathscr{G}$etting around upstate was much different from New York City. In the city, buses ran more often and/or you can take a train. Upstate: buses ran less frequent, no subway and it's harder to get a taxi during peak hours. Having a car would definitely be more convenient. I really did not think about driving because I could always get on a bus and/or train to go anywhere in the city.

Before I was born, my father used to drive, but after a car accident, he never drove again. I am not sure if my mother was afraid of driving, but she never learned after the accident.

My husband wanted me to learn how to drive and continually harassed me about doing so. For years, I was tormented by verbal abuse, threats, things withheld and taken from me, until I learned how to drive.

I wondered "Why didn't he want to drive?" "Why me?" With the way he was acting with money, how we were going to pay for the expenses of owning and maintaining a car? Even if I did learn, with his behavior, it was just not a good idea.

Years later, I gave in and learned how to drive. I thought if I did this, maybe my husband would act differently towards me. What a deceptive thought. Months later, someone gave us a used car. He let other people and a woman he was having an affair with, drive him around on his drug missions. While he rode off in the car, I walked to work. The stress and heartbreak of these episodes caused me to go into depression and my hair began to break off and fall out. So distraught over his treatment of me, especially after complying with his demand to drive, suicidal thoughts began to torment me.

While driving down the street, I heard a voice whisper to me, "Why don't you end it all now?" Tears began running down my face and my heart started beating fast. I wanted to crash the car and I was looking for something to run into without hurting anyone else. I started praying and crying out to God, while thoughts of my children and the consequences of suicide, raced through my mind.

Suddenly, I felt the peace of God come over me and I began to calm down. When I came to the next corner, I made a right turn, went back home and parked the car. I was so thankful that I did not kill myself. Not long after that, the car broke down and we did not get another car for almost nine years.

MUTED BY FEAR

Can I speak?
I think about it,
But I'm afraid,
Should I say that now?
I don't think I should,
I wish I could!
What about how I feel?
I think about it,
But how would they react?
If I open my mouth,
Would it just be slapped?

-----Shut....Up!-----

You can't say that!
They don't care,
Why waste your time?
You know you fear.
Fear their actions, reactions, the pain of it all,
If you open your mouth,
This time,
How hard will their hand fall?
Muted by fear,
Can't tell no one,
Can't hold it no longer!
I gotta let it out!
When, how, or who?
Can I let it out to?

Chapter 12

<u>FEAR, BLAME AND ANGER</u>

For years we lived in two family houses. The last one we moved into, the tenant upstairs was a very quiet, older woman. After several years, she moved out and a young man who worked most of the time, moved in. There was very little noise, so we were fine with him living above us. When he left, the new tenants were so noisy, until it pushed us into moving out.

My husband knew another landlord who had a house for rent on the same block. Renting this house was going to cost $250 more per month. He promised to help pay the rent, since he was now receiving an income from disability and SSI. When that time came, all I heard was excuses why he could not give me the money. The full amount fell on me and it made things even harder on us.

I continued to try to make the relationship work; still praying, still believing, and still waiting for change. We tried to do things as a family; watching movies, barbecues in the backyard and going out to eat. On Super Bowl Sundays, Memorial Day, 4th of July and Labor Day, he invited friends over to eat. There were more glimmers of hope, mixed with sporadic drug use.

The first Christmas Eve we spent in the house started out with dinner and then a movie. I was thinking, *this is nice*, but still had a feeling that something was going to happen. Unfortunately, around the holidays, something usually goes wrong. So after the movie, the children went upstairs. My husband and I started talking, and he said something that I disagreed with. He did not want to hear what I had to say about the situation.

I don't remember why there was a belt downstairs, but he started yelling and his anger intensified. He said that if I said another word that he was going to hit me. He picked up the belt and said, "Say something else!"

*I did not feel it was fair that he could say anything he wanted to and I could not, for fear of being hurt. God was strengthening me, and little by little I was getting the boldness to stand up for myself.

So I said what I believe I had a right to say, and he swung the belt, hitting my thigh. He swung it again, daring me to say another word. The hits bruised my thigh in two places. I did not say anything else (mute) because of fear. If I opened my mouth again, I did not know where else he would hit me with the belt.

*I stood up for myself but it was at the expense of being hurt. Even though it was unfair for me not to be able to express how I felt, it became dangerous to test my abuser. He was stuck in the emotion of anger through the unresolved issues he suffered in his past. The effects of crack cocaine on his brain, just made things worse.

STUCK

I'm stuck in hurt and pain!
Stuck, cause it hurts so bad,
It has made me mad.
Mad enough to hurt,
And inflict pain,
On those whom I say I love and should help,
I just can't control myself.
Haven't admitted yet,
That I need help.
I'm stuck in my hurt and pain!
I just can't seem to move past,
My Past.
I'm stuck,
Don't know how to deal,
With these emotions and impulses, I feel.
Gotta find something to medicate them,
A drink, a needle or a smoke on a stem.
So I won't have to deal,
with this pain that's so real.
I've suffered abuse,
Rejection and hurt,
Now I'm stuck right there,
Not knowing how to heal.
I'm stuck,
How can my life turn around?
I've got to do something,
But it's so hard,
In the meantime, I'm losing,
The ones that I love.

I cried as low as I could because I did not want the children to hear me crying. However, they heard us arguing, and he left. I sat downstairs for a while trying to get myself together. One of my children came halfway down the steps and asked if he did something to me. I played it off because I did not want to tell them what happened.

After that altercation, I was not feeling the holiday spirit at all. He came back later and apologized, but it did not matter. My tolerance level was diminishing. At this point, him saying sorry, translated in my mind as him wanting to keep me imprisoned in his world.

BLAME

Adam blamed Eve,
You blame me,
Who did it?
You did it!
How could *I* have put *You* through it?
When it was *You* who chose to do it!
It was your choice to pick up the stem,
Time and time again!
Dreams, money, trust and love,
Up in smoke!
And *You* blame me?
When *I* prayed and fasted,
You ran and resisted.
When you went in for help,
You bailed out by yourself.
Locked up in prisons,
Because of your choices and missions,
But *You* blame me?
When will you stop listening to those voices?
And start making better choices!
You blame me?
For not protecting and having your back,
What about me?
I'm unprotected,
How should *I* feel about that?
Need to put an end to this blaming madness,
The hurt, the pain and the sadness.
I call the police,
You blame me,

Am I supposed to suffer, continuously?
No!
Now *You,* take the responsibility.

In 2010, I was on my way to work after an appointment. As I was walking to the bus stop in the rain, I slipped and heard a popping sound in my right ankle. After spraining my ankle so many times before, I knew this was more than a sprain.

As I sat on the ground in pain, the bus came. I was too scared to get up and put weight on my ankle. The people at the bus stop, turned and looked at me, then got on the bus. One young man, stopped and asked if I wanted him to call an ambulance for me, before he boarded the bus. Thank God, he did. The ambulance came quick. I felt like I was about to pass out. The paramedics started asking me all the usual questions; my name, the date and day, but I could barely get the answers out. I was going into a state of shock because of the trauma to my ankle.

At the hospital, the x-ray showed a diagonal fracture in my right ankle. I was placed in a cast all the way up to my knee and had to keep it on for almost eight weeks. I was hopping up the stairs and sliding down the stairs on my backside. I was not able to go back to work for about four months, but God provided for us. My husband helped a lot around the house, I was truly thankful to God for that. These are the times that kept me holding on, hoping he was going to stop for good. However, there were still episodes of drug use.

In February of the next year, my husband really pushed the idea of getting a car again. He said I should not be walking so much after breaking my ankle. I told him I did not want to be treated like before. He assured me, it would be different this time, and I did not have to worry.

Having the car was OK in the beginning, but it quickly turned into a nightmare. My husband began arguing, using profanity and complaining because he did not like the way I was driving. I had to: park where *he* wanted me to park, take the route *he* wanted me to take and go where he wanted to go, even if I didn't feel like it. I drove on pins, needles, and eggshells when he was with me. He threatened to have someone else drive the car, again. The verbal/emotional abuse and anger increased and intensified. I began to cry out to God to deliver me out of this nightmare.

Before September, on our way home from church, the car broke down. We did not have the money to fix it, so it sat in the driveway. The person who sold us the car, let us use another one and told us we could pay for it during income tax time the next year. We were back on the road; the verbal abuse started again, the uncomfortable and nervous feelings came back.

A few months later, preoccupied with thoughts of the college work (B.A. early childhood courses I just started), I had an accident. My husband and two daughters were in the car with me and we were leaving Taco Bell. While turning left, I hit the front left side of an SUV, causing minor damage to the driver's car. The right side of the front bumper of our car was dented in. It did not look bad to me and was still drivable. The driver of the SUV was not injured, and after the exchange of insurance information, I never heard from her again. My husband and daughters said they were fine. I felt pain in my thigh, the left side of my neck and back.

My husband was angry and complained about how ugly the dent looked on the front bumper of the car. He constantly reminded me that the accident was my fault and would not let me live it down. We did not have collision coverage, so it could not be fixed until we had enough money. He acted like he did not care that I was injured, nor how I felt about the accident.

*I believe that the addiction and other unresolved personal issues, caused him to value drugs and things more than his family.

Because of the injuries, I could not continue working with infants and toddlers. We had to live on disability pay from the job, car insurance (loss wages) and AFLAC.

Seven months after the accident, I began to feel better and started thinking about what type of work I was going to do now. While thinking about that, my husband and I decided to sell the old car in the driveway to fix the front bumper. The car was taken to the repair shop on a Friday and was finished the next day. On Sunday we drove to church (with the new bumper) and back home.

Later on that afternoon, I decided to drive to Wal-Mart and pick up a few things. On route to the store, a young woman, driving a minivan, came out of a parking lot. As she entered the road from the left, she hit the back wheel of my car. Now this time, it was not my fault. I lost control of the car, hit a fire hydrant (knocking it off its base), thinking the car would stop. I dragged the fire hydrant and the new bumper, several feet under my car, before stopping on the opposite side of the road.

It felt surreal, and I was thinking, "I wish this was a nightmare that I could wake up from." I prayed, "God, please let this car stop, don't let me hit anyone," as I steered it over to the other side of the street. Thank God, I did not see any cars coming in either direction and was able to stop safely.

I got out and looked at the front. The new bumper was dragging under the front of the car. The fire hydrant stuck underneath, slightly elevated the car. All types of car fluids were leaking onto the street. I looked at the left side and saw the damage to the area around the back wheel. My car was totaled. The young woman came over to me and asked if I was alright. I said I was (at the time), and asked her; What was she doing? Why didn't she see me? She had no explanation.

When I got back in my car, all the pain hit me and I started feeling horrible. I put my head down in pain, feeling like I was about to pass out. Soon after, an officer came to the car and asked if I needed to go to the hospital, I painfully said "Yes." The ambulance came and took me to the hospital.

They x-rayed my chest and neck area. There was nothing damaged or broken, Thank God. However, the left side of my neck and back were re-injured. There was also a slight injury to the rotator cuff in my right shoulder. The crash also jarred my broken ankle, causing pain, again.

Although the x-ray showed no broken bones, they found spots on both lungs. I did not understand how I could have spots on my lungs and not have a problem breathing.

However, I remembered as a child, after any type of physical exertion (jumping rope, etc.) for a long period of time, upon breathing in, there was a funny feeling in my chest and I started coughing. I do not remember saying anything to my mother about it, so she never took me to the doctor to check it out. After resting for a while, I went back outside to play.

I'm thinking; my father smoked, so I was around second hand smoke, as a child; could that be the reason? I never smoked and whenever my husband did drugs or anything it was somewhere else. I wondered, where did these the spots come from and how long did I have them.

They sent me to a lung doctor and he scheduled a series of tests. Because of my breast cancer history, he said, "I will be surprised if it's not cancer." After the tests, they scheduled an operation to remove a small section of the left lung and a lymph node from the middle of my chest, for a biopsy.

A month before the operation, my husband started arguing with me about all kinds of things; including wrecking the car and our oldest daughter. The more we argued, the angrier he became. He started cursing and making all kinds of threats; from hurting me and our daughter, to choking me to death.

He stood over me, while I was lying in the bed (afraid to sit up) with his hand raised to hit me. I reached for the phone, he dared me to call the police. When I looked at his face, his eyes, seemed like they were popping out of his head. All I could see was anger and the evil things that were controlling him. At that point, it sounded like whatever in him that hated me, was talking. God gave me the courage to call the police and I said to myself, whatever happens, happens. I can't keep living like this.

I was just in an accident, about to have surgery on my lungs, so if I die, I won't have to worry about anything.

As I dialed the police, he snatched the phone out of my hand. I heard the dispatcher say "hello", before it hit the floor and the battery popped out. He went downstairs, I put the battery back in the phone and it rang immediately. The dispatcher was calling me back. I was then able to tell her what happened and within minutes the police came to the house. They arrested him for interfering with an attempt to make an emergency phone call, which is a violation of state law.

I filed a refraining order against him, which took a lot of courage. He could be around me, but could not aggravate, hit, harass or threaten me. I was too afraid to file for a full order of protection at that time.

Three weeks later, they operated on me. I stayed in the hospital for five days and came home on Father's Day. He asked me if I was going to go out to dinner with him. I looked at him like he was crazy and said "No". I did not feel like going anywhere but to bed. I could hardly speak above a whisper (common with the procedure), in pain, tired, hungry, fluid still draining from the left side of my chest, and having a problem breathing. He left me laying there and went out to eat for Father's Day. My oldest daughter went out and got something for me to eat.

The results of the biopsy and resection showed that I had Sarcoidosis (information on the web) in my lungs, which is an auto-immune disease. I was not happy with that diagnosis, but thank God it was not cancer as the doctor previously believed.

R U LISTENING?

Do you see?
Do you hear?
R u listening?
When I scream!
I'm screaming, STOP!
I'm screaming, CARE!
I'm screaming, LOVE!
I'm screaming, UNDERSTAND!
I'm screaming, I'M TIRED!
I'm screaming, I'M HURTING!
I'm screaming, CHANGE!
I'm screaming, I CAN'T DO THIS ANYMORE!
But you don't hear,
Doesn't seem like you even care!
So, I'm *GONE!*

Chapter 13

THE WAITING IS OVER

After the diagnosis of Sarcoidosis, the scenario of the accidents and the incident of my husband threatening my life, played over and over in my mind. I began to think about my age, health, the effects of the trauma on the children and our future. I could not see myself or the children living another year, month, week or day like this.

In the midst of another argument, I told him to leave. We talked about separation and divorce, many times, so this was not something new or a surprise to him. The waiting was over; this was *my* "enough" moment.

He left and found a room down the street. He continued coming back to the house, arguing and harassing me. My husband was so angry with me because at this point in his life, it was hard for him to settle into another place. I began to pray for things to settle down, for his peace and stability. I needed to start the healing process in my mind, body, and emotions.

He finally went into a recovery program. I was hoping he would stick to it and change. However, several months later when he called, I heard the demanding and controlling tone that he used to manipulate me for years. He said he was coming back to the house to stay for a week or more and that was it. At that moment, I froze. I could not move for a few minutes and tears began to run down my face. I felt vulnerable, hopeless and helpless, fearing this will never end. I did not argue the point, because I was mentally, emotionally and physically drained. My "no" still meant nothing to him, I had no say in the matter.

He stayed for the whole month in my son's room. It felt awkward; tense, uncomfortable, and a bit scary. We did not get into any serious arguments. With much prayer, God helped me through it. In the beginning of the next month he found an apartment.

On the sixth of that month, he came over, asking for five dollars to get his clothes washed. He reminded me that his birthday was coming up. I gave him the five dollars, and he was calm at that point. I had already spoke to our youngest son about giving his father something for his birthday earlier. We were just waiting for a ride to the store so he could cash his check, before his father came over.

My husband became more restless, walking in and out of the room complaining. It seemed like he still was upset about the whole scenario of having to leave the house. The argument escalated into him cursing and blaming me for all kinds of things. He then said, "Keep the money" and threw the five dollars on the bed. I put the money in my pocket. I asked him what did he want from me, and he said, "I want everything you have." He kept repeating, "Till death do us part", as he walked down the stairs.

I told my son that I had to get out of the house, because I felt something bad was about to happen. I told him I was leaving, but he wanted to wait for a ride. As I started down the stairs, my husband was coming up. He swung his hand, hitting me and said, "Move!"

With the restraining order in place, I could have called the police many times before, but I was afraid. He said repeatedly that he hated me and wanted me dead. This made it more frightening to wait.

I knew he was angry and could not understand how I felt. After all these years of sacrificing and suffering through countless stressful, traumatizing episodes and events, things were still unstable. Regardless of what happened, the consequences of his actions or help, he never stopped using drugs completely. Since he did not want to change his behaviors, I refused to wait any longer.

I continuously forgave him, then tolerated the verbal and emotional abuse over and over again. Going through an episode of his drug use and another cycle of losing things, was just too much to handle. I refused to live with the arguing, cursing, name calling, angry outbursts, fear, worry, stress and control, another minute. The children expressed to me how unhappy they were and wanted to leave because of the destructive behaviors.

I felt, if I did not call this time, it would just continue and possibly get worse.

I said, "I'm calling the police," but I really did not want to. So I went to the door to try to leave and my husband stepped in front of me and locked it. There was a crazy look in his eyes. I walked into the living room and as I dialed 911, he snatched the phone out of my hand. Then, when I picked up the house phone, we struggled and he took it out of my hand. I quickly went to the back door to try to leave; as I opened it, he came behind me and shut it. After all the struggling and conflict; I leaned over the freezer near the back door trying to catch my breath. He stepped back and I heard him say in anger, "I wish you would drop dead."

I yelled to our youngest son, who was upstairs, to call the police. My husband went upstairs and took the cell phone out of his hand and began to argue with him. However, the call already went through. I went up behind him because I did not want him to hurt our son. When I said, "Leave him alone!" he turned and came after me yelling and cursing.

By this time, my oldest daughter had walked into the upstairs hallway and saw us in my room and she yelled, "Leave my mom alone." In his anger, he turned and started walking towards her yelling. I tried to stop him from touching her. As she walked into her room, he went through the doorway, behind her. She turned and faced him. When I tried to get in between them, he pushed me onto her bed. He backed up and she looked him in his eyes and screamed, "*You need to ask God to help you, because You need Help!*" He did not say or do anything else but turned and walked out of the room.

*I knew God was in the midst of this whole situation because it could have been real ugly and deadly.

When I got my phone back, it rang and the dispatcher at the police department was on the line. I told her what just happened and what he had on, just in case he left before they came. While I was on the phone, he came back towards me still very angry and said, "Give me the five dollars," (I put back in my pocket earlier). He reached in my pocket, snatched the money as I said, "Leave me alone," and then he left. The dispatcher heard the altercation and said that the police were on the way. They arrived in time to see him walking across the street and arrested him. Another officer came into the house to talk to us.

By now, I am breathing harder, heart beating faster, and about to pass out, so they called an ambulance. I did not want to go to the hospital; I wanted to get things taken care of with the police. I really felt sorry it had to end this way.

*It is sad and disturbing to know that addictive behaviors, and abuse have and are still tearing,

countless numbers of families apart. There are many different dysfunctional scenarios. With some couples, both will be fighting each other and/or using drugs. Sometimes the woman dominates the man.

*Each situation must be handled differently, but the outcome is nevertheless traumatizing to those who are going through it. Since there are various types of temperaments/tolerance levels and personalities; a situation, one person will tolerate and or be afraid to leave, another person will not tolerate it and leave quick. No matter what kind or degree of dysfunctional scenario it may be, it is not good for anyone to live in that environment.

While he was in prison, I filed for a divorce. I began to get myself physically, mentally and emotionally together.

*Sometimes you have to let go of someone in order for change to happen. We are incapable of changing anyone. I found that out the long, hard way.

After his release from prison, he has been in contact with his daughters and oldest son. He is trying to build a new relationship with them. I am happy to see this happening. I pray that they are healed by resolving issues they have with him and in turn he will heal also. I truly pray a new beginning for him and that these will be the best years of his life.

Chapter 14

<u>CONCLUDING THOUGHTS</u>

The question is, "When is enough, enough?" Everyone has his or her breaking point, but unfortunately, that breaking point can end in hospitalization or death. Not everyone gets out of domestic violence situations without sacrificing their lives and/or losing loved ones. We were not born to be beaten, cursed out, threatened, harassed, terrorized and victimized; but cared for and loved.

If you are already in a relationship with someone who is an addict, abuser, and/or unfaithful, it is your choice to stay or leave. You do not have to feel like a failure, if you have to let go, especially when you have tried everything possible to make it work.

Please do not stay stuck in the unhealthy relationship. Do not miss any God-given opportunity and/or if you see a way and time, to safely escape. Find someone you can trust with wisdom, can pray effectually for you and help you find the solution to your situation.

Before entering another relationship, it is important to work on *you*. Do not allow past hurts and bad relationship to spoil or destroy your chances of having a healthy and happy relationship/marriage. You must confront and resolve the issues and pain of your past. Don't expect the next person to fix your problems. Please make sure you are not trying to fix theirs.

When I married my ex-husband, it was emotionally driven by loneliness. We should have never been married on the basis of looks and feelings. They were a trap and a mask to disguise the underlying dysfunctional issues, that eventually sabotaged the marriage.

Emotional-driven attraction to an individual should never be the deciding factor for marriage, especially when drugs or other dysfunctional behaviors are present.

A year prior to us separating, we renewed our vows, hoping that it would change things. However, nothing changed because the underlying issues were not dealt with. I wanted him to stop using drugs for the sake of his health, to save our marriage and the relationship with the children.

My ex-husband did some positive things with and for his children and instilled in them some valuable skills. Unfortunately, the addiction limited those occurrences. I know things would have been better for them, if they were taken out of the dysfunctional environment sooner. Nevertheless, I am truly blessed to have four awesome children.

Regardless of our poor choices, God still showed us His love, compassion, mercy, and faithfulness. He is the one that can turn things around for our good.

Abusers will blame you for their abusive behavior towards you and the wrong they are responsible for. They are deceived to believe that it is always someone else's fault. You may start believing that it is your fault, by their continual accusations against you.

The abuser becomes paranoid and jealous of the people you associate with. They will: strip you of your identity and self-esteem making you feel like a failure, stupid, weak, ashamed and embarrassed, isolate you from your family, friends and others who can help because they do not want to lose control over you. This is unhealthy and unsafe.

Their anger rises if they find out you told anyone about what they did or said to you and/or the children. You stop going places or talking with others, because of fear.

Addicts and abusers need help, but they may not admit it. There had to be something, someone, somewhere, at some time in their lives that caused them to become dysfunctional. They are hurting/feeling emotional pain and unfortunately, do not know how to properly express/handle it. Medicating the problem, lashing out and/or blaming others, becomes the alternative to, dealing with their issues and getting help. My prayer is; they want and find help for themselves and be healed.

96

HEAL THE PAIN OF MY PAST

Struggling to love once more,
After my heart has been broken before,
Heal the pain of my past.
Torn by guilt and regret,
Help me to forgive and forget,
Heal the pain of my past.
I've been betrayed by a man,
Help me to trust again,
Heal the pain of my past.
I know there's a better future for me,
Lord, set me free,
Free from the pain of my past!

Chapter 15

THE HEALING PROCESS BEGINS

How was I going to recover, after 20+ years of trauma and emotional abuse? Where would I start? In order for me to heal, I had to focus on myself. This was difficult, since all my time and energy went into trying to please and change another person. It was hard to think about what I wanted or needed. Nevertheless, I knew it was time to take care of myself; otherwise I would remain a victim.

I already was weak in faith because of the repeated traumatic situations. Negativity and low self-esteem was very strong but I had to start somewhere. Through the help of my church leader, I began to make my way out of the depths of a life oppression, control, manipulation and abuse.

I believe that we are spiritual beings, housed in a body and we have a soul that is made up of our mind, will, intellect, and emotions. My body and soul were affected by the stress of living in a dysfunctional relationship for decades. It contributed to the development of sicknesses and diseases in my body. My soul suffered depression, anxiety, grief and loss; my mind replayed all the traumatic events.

I kept seeing and hearing the anger in him. The recorded verbal abuse of cursing, yelling, disrespectful and demeaning remarks played continuously in my head throughout the day. I went through mood swings, crying and grieving over a failed relationship I had worked so hard to fix and save. I felt like I had just lost a loved one. The truth is, I did.

I believe God uses other people to help us to get through the pain so I began counseling sessions. Counseling helped me focus on, separating myself from the fear, and the unhealthy co-dependent relationship and feelings that controlled me for so many years. Going through counseling was intense and emotional agony, as I worked through very painful memories of the marriage. I attended sessions with a domestic violence social worker at the YWCA and a trauma group at a counseling center. Continuing through the process, I began to sort out how the abuse made me feel (as my church leader taught me). I am still coming to a resolve about it all.

Another part of my recovery was dealing with the affects it had on my children. Thoughts of guilt and regret for allowing it to last as long as it did, ran through my mind continuously.

My role as the protecting, shielding, buffering and compensating parent had to shift to the disciplinarian, which was unfamiliar to me. My daughters expressed that they saw me as weak, because I allowed their father to take advantage of me for so long. They also expressed their anger and hurt because they felt I did not protect or provide for them properly. I asked them to forgive me for the pain I allowed them to go through.

I now have to establish myself as the head of the house, set order, be firm and enforce rules. This literally became a battle of power. I needed to gain self-esteem, confidence and a strong perception of myself being the one in charge. I began to tell myself, "I have the authority they don't." "I am the authority, they are not."

With the help of prayer, counseling, and instructions, I am gaining the confidence and personal strength to use my God-given authority in many areas. This is an ongoing process, but it is changing and strengthening my relationship with my daughters. I told them they have to forgive, stop blaming me, and begin to resolve the issues, in order to put it in the past.

My sons are going through their own way of healing, but they have been very supportive and glad that I am moving on with my life. I am truly grateful for another chance to be happy! Better and greater is ahead and I must pursue it!

The healing process continues...

SEE YOURSELF

See yourself, not dying,
See yourself, getting better,
See yourself, striving for greater.
See yourself, not taking it anymore,
See yourself, loving, caring and trusting,
See yourself, making wise choices.
See yourself, taking care of you,
See yourself, pursuing and living your dreams,
See yourself, exercising your gifts and talents.
See yourself, in a better place,
Emotionally, mentally, physically and financially,
See yourself, being who God says you are,
Start now!
Start by seeing yourself!
Then BE
BE the one that lives your dreams!

DESTINY CALLS

Destiny Calls,
But I don't hear,
My ears are deaf,
By so much fear.
Destiny Calls,
Don't know how I will
Answer the call,
This nightmare is *Real*!
Destiny still Calls,
The voice is now faint,
The bricks in the wall,
Are starting to fall.
Destiny Calls,
I'm making moves,
In pursuit of change,
And something new.
Destiny calls,
Now I see and hear,
It was never too far,
It was always near.
Voices had to be shut up!
Activities shut down!
Mindsets had to change!
People had to leave!
To hear the call of
My Destiny!

ALL IS NOT LOST

All is not lost,
There's so much more in store,
All is not lost,
There are more open doors.
All is not lost,
Just what you didn't need!
All is not lost,
Even if it brought you pain and grief,
All is not lost,
Because God is bringing you relief.
All is not lost,
There's more love, more joy,
More laughter, more peace,
And more prosperity.
All is not lost!
There's BETTER coming to YOU!

For those who desire spiritual help
Special Prayers

God, help me to wait on you and acknowledge you in all my moves, for you know what's best for me.

Father, forgive me for what I have done and help me to get out of this situation.

Father, forgive them for what they have done to me and help me to forgive them and myself.

God, please take the mental and emotional pain away, so I can function correctly and take care of myself and my family.

Lord, give me strength and wisdom to make the right decision at the right time.

Father, I thank you for your provisions, help and strength.

Thank you for healing me of all the diseases that have attacked my body, thank you for making me whole.

ANGER

Lord I have a lot of hurt and pain due to rejection, neglect, abandonment, all types of abuse, grief and loss which have resulted in unresolved issues. It has caused me to hurt myself by engaging in self destructive behaviors (drugs, alcohol, etc.) and hurt others (family friends and enemies). I ask you to forgive me and help me to forgive those who hurt me, hurt/killed family members/friends, so I will be able to release these feelings to be free to love, care, and be kind to others Amen.

Declarations

I declare that God made me somebody, I am valuable, beautifully and wonderfully made and worth much to Him, myself and my family!
I declare that God my father is the greater one that's inside me and He is going to get me through this!
I declare that God has made me more than a conqueror and He loves me in Jesus name!
I declare that God is working things out for my good, and I declare that I love Him and know that he has a purpose for my life!
I declare that All is well and getting Better in Jesus Name!

Scriptures

Here's just a few scriptures that have helped me and they continue to strengthen and encourage me. I pray they do the same for you.

All Scriptures below are written in the King James Version

King James Version (Crown copyright/Public Domain in the United States)

Isaiah 40:29-31 He giveth power to the faint; and to them that have no might he increaseth strength.
30 Even the youths shall faint and be weary, and the young men shall utterly fall:
31 But they that wait upon the LORD shall renew their strength; they shall mount up with wings as eagles; they shall run, and not be weary; and they shall walk, and not faint.

Isaiah 41:10-13,17
10 Fear thou not; for I am with thee: be not dismayed; for I am thy God: I will strengthen thee; yea, I will help thee; yea, I will uphold thee with the right hand of my righteousness.
11 Behold, all they that were incensed against thee shall be ashamed and confounded: they shall be as nothing; and they that strive with thee shall perish.

12 Thou shalt seek them, and shalt not find them, even them that contended with thee: they that war against thee shall be as nothing, and as a thing of nought.
13 For I the LORD thy God will hold thy right hand, saying unto thee, Fear not; I will help thee.
17 When the poor and needy seek water, and there is none, and their tongue faileth for thirst, I the LORD will hear them, I the God of Israel will not forsake them.

Isaiah 43:18,19
18 Remember ye not the former things, neither consider the things of old.
19 Behold, I will do a new thing; now it shall spring forth; shall ye not know it? I will even make a way in the wilderness, and rivers in the desert.

Isaiah 54:5-8,11-15,17
5 For thy Maker is thine husband; the LORD of hosts is his name; and thy Redeemer the Holy One of Israel; The God of the whole earth shall he be called.
6 For the LORD hath called thee as a woman forsaken and grieved in spirit, and a wife of youth, when thou wast refused, saith thy God.
7 For a small moment have I forsaken thee; but with great mercies will I gather thee.
8 In a little wrath I hid my face from thee for a moment; but with everlasting kindness will I have mercy on thee, saith the LORD thy Redeemer.

11 O thou afflicted, tossed with tempest, and not comforted, behold, I will lay thy stones with fair colours, and lay thy foundations with sapphires.

12 And I will make thy windows of agates, and thy gates of carbuncles, and all thy borders of pleasant stones.

13 And all thy children shall be taught of the Lord; and great shall be the peace of thy children.

14 In righteousness shalt thou be established: thou shalt be far from oppression; for thou shalt not fear: and from terror; for it shall not come near thee.

15 Behold, they shall surely gather together, but not by me: whosoever shall gather together against thee shall fall for thy sake.

17 No weapon that is formed against thee shall prosper; and every tongue that shall rise against thee in judgment thou shalt condemn. This is the heritage of the servants of the Lord, and their righteousness is of me, saith the Lord.

Psalms 35:1-10

1 Plead my cause, O Lord, with them that strive with me: fight against them that fight against me.

2 Take hold of shield and buckler, and stand up for mine help.

3 Draw out also the spear, and stop the way against them that persecute me: say unto my soul, I am thy salvation.

4 Let them be confounded and put to shame that seek after my soul: let them be turned back and brought to confusion that devise my hurt.

5 Let them be as chaff before the wind: and let the angel of the LORD chase them.

6 Let their way be dark and slippery: and let the angel of the LORD persecute them.

7 For without cause have they hid for me their net in a pit, which without cause they have digged for my soul.

8 Let destruction come upon him at unawares; and let his net that he hath hid catch himself: into that very destruction let him fall.

9 And my soul shall be joyful in the LORD: it shall rejoice in his salvation.

10 All my bones shall say, LORD, who is like unto thee, which deliverest the poor from him that is too strong for him, yea, the poor and the needy from him that spoileth him?

Psalm 139:14
I will praise thee; for I am fearfully and wonderfully made: marvellous are thy works; and that my soul knoweth right well.

II Corinthians 10:3-6
3 For though we walk in the flesh, we do not war after the flesh:

4 (For the weapons of our warfare are not carnal, but mighty through God to the pulling down of strong holds;)

5 Casting down imaginations, and every high thing that exalteth itself against the knowledge of God, and bringing into captivity every thought to the obedience of Christ;

6 And having in a readiness to revenge all disobedience, when your obedience is fulfilled.

Philippians 1:6
Being confident of this very thing, that he which hath begun a good work in you will perform it until the day of Jesus Christ:

Isaiah 49:24-25
24 Shall the prey be taken from the mighty, or the lawful captive delivered?

25 But thus saith the LORD, Even the captives of the mighty shall be taken away, and the prey of the terrible shall be delivered: for I will contend with him that contendeth with thee, and I will save thy children.

Proverbs 3:5-6
5 Trust in the LORD with all thine heart; and lean not unto thine own understanding.

6 In all thy ways acknowledge him, and he shall direct thy paths.

Jeremiah 31:3
The LORD hath appeared of old unto me, saying, Yea, I have loved thee with an everlasting love: therefore, with lovingkindness have I drawn thee.

Jeremiah 17:14

Heal me, O LORD, and I shall be healed; save me, and I shall be saved: for thou art my praise.

1 John 1:9

If we confess our sins, he is faithful and just to forgive us our sins, and to cleanse us from all unrighteousness.

Lamentation 3:22-26

22 It is of the LORD's mercies that we are not consumed, because his compassions fail not.

23 They are new every morning: great is thy faithfulness.

24 The LORD is my portion, saith my soul; therefore, will I hope in him.

25 The LORD is good unto them that wait for him, to the soul that seeketh him.

26 It is good that a man should both hope and quietly wait for the salvation of the LORD.

Bibliography

Merriam-Webster's Collegiate Dictionary. 11th ed. Springfield, MA: Merriam-Webster, 2003. Also available athttp://www.merriam-webster.com/.

Scripture quotations taken from the Amplified® Bible, Copyright © 2015 by The Lockman Foundation. Used by permission." (www.Lockman.org)

HOTLINES:

National Suicide Pevention Hotline
1-800-273-TALK (8255) [24/7 hotline]
1-888-628-9454 (Spanish)
1-800-799-4889 (TTY)

National Domestic Violence Hotline
1-800-799-7233 or 1-800-787-3224 (TTY)

National Sexual Assault Hotline
1-800-656-4673 [24/7 hotline]

Hopeline
Phone: 800-442-HOPE (4673)

National Center for Posttraumatic Stress Disorder
Phone: 802-296-6300

National Drug and Alcohol Treatment Hotline –
Treatment referrals
Phone: 800-662-HELP (4357)

S.A.F.E. Alternatives
Phone: 800-DONTCUT (800-366-8288)

Please check out your local community resources for assistance with domestic violence issues, professional counseling agencies and legal assistance. Get help and be safe!

Your Personal Notes

Your Personal Notes

Your Personal Notes

Your Personal Notes

CPSIA information can be obtained
at www.ICGtesting.com
Printed in the USA
FFOW05n2201220316